CRACKED
&
BROKEN

---

poems of midlife

Sean Petrie

Burlwood Books

Burlwood Books

Austin, Texas
BurlwoodBooks.com

First published in the United States of America
by Burlwood Books 2023

Front cover design by Andrea Wofford
Back cover design by Andrea Wofford & Shanna Gerlach

Front cover illustration from French magazine *L'Illustration*, No 2481,
September 13, 1890, titled "The Patrie hot air balloon falling 1400 metres,
Paris, France," housed in the museum Biblioteca Ambrosiana, Milan, Italy
(artist unknown)
Back cover photo by Brad Marcum

ISBN 978-1-961853-00-3

1. Poetry 2. Aging—Poetry

To the regulars at The Gingerman & Elliott Bay,
and all the other soul searchers out there

Also to my parents
(I'm doing fine, Mom & Dad, I promise)

Contents

Nothing knows how shining and vital you are.

—T.R. HUMMER

You Are a Child of the Universe

Be gentle
With your old dreams
Be kind
To that voice of panic

We all need a hug
In the dark

We all
Need

And it never stops
Which is a good thing

Be kind to those broken dreams
Be gentle with yourself
You are strong enough
To take it.

MILLSTONE

"I remember tomorrow so vividly,"
Said the old man at the Irish pub
At least that's what I imagined
His words meant
I couldn't understand a single one
He was just a jumble of drunken Gaelic
With huge gray hairs tufting from his ears
You could have set a piece of cheese there
Was a thought I had

We closed down the bar, me and old ear cheese, Seamus
(I learned his name from the bartender)
Along with the bartender and his friend
At two in the morning the constable came by
And we hid in the dark, all four of us,
While the flashlight searched empty barstools from the window
Then we resumed drinking
Seamus becoming louder and less telligible
With each round of Kilbeggan's
Until at last, the bartender said,
"All right, Seamus, it's time"
The three of them shuffled down a hall
Behind the bar

I followed
And found them in a tiny room with a cot
Where Seamus had settled onto his back
While the other two hoisted a wheel-shaped stone
Onto his chest

"Old millstone," the bartender explained
"Makes it so he don't get up in the night,
Wander around, piss in the corner."

From beneath his stone
Seamus smiled
And gave me a thumbs up

And I wandered home alone
In the dark
Wondering what was keeping me
In place.

CELEBRATING

Mediocre donuts
Still
I eat them.

Barnacle (To What End?)

There are plenty of odes
To wrens and roses
But the barnacle
Goes noticed only in wrinkly noses
Perhaps a chuckle at the syllables, but no more

Still, take a moment
Kneel by the gray rock
See the cluster of star shells
Pick one, just one
See the patterns and pockets
The pimply bumps
Look closer, longer
There—a swirl of light
A dance of darkness and depth
Of clinging
To whatever is
Of being washed clean
Over and over
Of clustering together
With others of your kind
And to what end?
Yes
Simply there in the sun, salt, and sea
Simply alive and not caring
One star
Whether poems are written
In your honor

And to what end?
Yes.

I FIND IT HELPFUL

We are eating lunch
Deviled eggs and french fries
A decadent Friday
"How is your mom?" I ask
"She's been really depressed"
Is the response
And then a list of reasons why

But I do not hear them, not really
All I can think is
How her mom, Eileen, is always so cheerful
The rock of the family
As I dip another french fry in whatever
This delicious sauce is
And try to hide
How I am suddenly cheered
By her pain

(Later I will realize
It is because it gives me hope)

I find it helpful to know
None of us have shiny perfect lives
Or lies
Even with the kids and grandkids
Partner and spouse
Good job and good house
All the "shoulds" checked off her list
That I have not checked off mine
Even with all those boxes filled
Eileen still gets the blues

I should feel guilty
That the french fry
Tastes even better now
But I do not—
I am not alone.

LETTING THE GRAY GROW

I saw a picture of Alan Watts
From the 1970s
I had no idea who he was
Just a face in a poetry newsletter

He couldn't have been much different
Than my age now
But he had let the beard flourish
In a waterfall of white and black
The silvery strands at the temples
Flowing out like the straps of a hot air balloon
Unmoored

I have kept my face close-shaved
Every day since the gray cropped up
I have trimmed the sideburns
Higher and higher
I have tried not to be
Too revealing

But fuck it
That's what his face says to me
From decades ago
Fuck it and get in that balloon
Let the lines flail free
It's nobody's ride
But yours.

CARL

They say you are supposed to name your fear
That in the naming
Comes calming
Acceptance
Peace

Hello, Carl
That panic in the night
I shall call you this
That dread in the day
You shall henceforth be named
That unreturned text
That turbulent flight
That moment of deciding
Whether to open the door or stay in

Each frantic search on my phone
For some semblance of connection
Just one "like" on a post

Each moment in a crowd
When all the faces are turned
To each other or somewhere
Except mine

All this
You shall be Carl
And we shall try
To get through it
Together.

I Poured Out My Heart

Here at five thousand feet
Just after takeoff
I can see the city lights
The building right
Next
To yours

Are you looking up here?
This flash in the sky?
Probably not
You have probably moved on
Just like I should do

Still I crane my neck
Stretch to catch every last glimpse
Before you are gone.

"NO PHOTOS ALLOWED!"

My mom is laughing and swatting
Her hand like she's shooing a fly
But really it's at the camera—
At me taking the photo

I can almost hear that laugh
And her telling me
Not to try and capture life
But live it!

The best moments
Like supernovas
Are unrecorded and unwitnessed
Are not analyzed and re-lived
Like a photo of a long-dead star

You cannot capture a river
Just let it take you

But still we all do it
Dip a cup into the flow
Hoping when we sip it, later
It will still be as fresh

I can almost hear that laugh
Almost, but not quite
Which is just the way
My mom would want.

Vetiver Root

Mary Oliver knew—
Just put down the pen
Shut off the screen
Unhunch the shoulders and fingers

What else should you be doing?
The grass waves you forward
Soft fields for slow steps
Like there are snails underfoot
And there may be
This grass is tall
And flowing

Lie down
There is a reason
They extract its roots
For calming, soothing properties

Breathe deep
What else should you be doing?
With your slow, soft
Billowing life?

GROWING LETTUCE

Growing lettuce is poetry.
—Thich Nhat Hanh

I went to the art gallery
Again
Hoping to soak up inspiration

I read Robert McKee's *STORY*
Again
Almost finishing it this time

I bought the moleskin notebook
The brand new Mac
The color printer

Twenty years later
I finally took a walk
Nowhere in particular
I finally trusted
My own voice
Unfurling

That's when the life
Worth devouring
Finally came.

JIGGLY BITS

Whose sags are those?
How are they mine?
Whose bags are those?
That wrinkly line?

I swear just yesterday
I was so smooth!
Each time at the gym
I would improve!

But now my bits
Are jiggly and low
Where did the time
And firmness go?

I've tried to hide them
(My neck's the worst)
But bits want to jiggle
(They are well-rehearsed)

Is the answer to alter
Or cover my face?
No, to jiggle is to dance—
And I will embrace!

CRACKED

is a shell breaking is the only way to get the good stuff inside
whether squirrel nut or oyster or egg is the crunch underfoot of
moving forward always forward is saying yes always always yes
you cannot belong inside perfection is the new stretch of bones
is the couch creaking with freedom as you both rise

Bar Poems (a triptych)

I. Noticing

I have seen
The scraggled guy
Nursing his drink
The younger guy
Nursing his phone
Pretending

The friends laughing
With eyes glazed
Only for each other
The silent couple beside them
Glancing
With envy

The tired bartender
Forcing a smile
The sparks drifting
From drink to table to propped elbows
The unspoken sip of camaraderie
I wonder what they see
In me
Or if they even look

But hell yes they do—
That's why all of us
Are here.

II. Loneliness

It's his corner
Every night
Every pint
Every sip
Every smile
Some returned
Some at a memory
Only he sees.

III. Know the Center

Walk in—
The warm light steadies
The empty spot welcomes
Your leaning elbows, searching eyes
Straggling soul

Some need gyms
Some need oceans
Some need a cozy couch
Or moonlight hand-holding

But for now, this place
Full of mostly strangers
For now, this place
Is where your spinning
Stops.

INUNDATED WITH WONDER

A rainbow every morning who would pause to look at?
—Charles Scott Sherrington

I watched the short film
Luckily it was under 6 minutes
I mean who has time
For more than that?

The artist had taken some paint
Oils I think
A dollop of vermillion and cerulean blue
And then the tiniest bit of white
Added with a microscopic dropper
The kind you would see injected
Into a Petri dish

And then the high-powered lens zoomed in
Closer and closer
Countries were crafted—
Here was Oceania
Surrounded by billowing seas
Planets were born in real-time
The swirls of red-orange clouds
Deep-blue filigrees
The same as Jupiter must have been
In the early days
And then galaxies streamed
Across my tiny phone screen
So close I could feel myself plummeting
Through them

I had to sit down

All that
In a drop of paint

Nearby a hummingbird floated
On the breeze.

You Can't

Have everything, my therapist says

But my therapist is not here
In the early morning
When I fall through the cracks
  Of loves not embraced
  Of jobs not quit
  Of the photo never taken—

The one showing me at the seaside house
Of my dreams
Showing my partner, mouth wide in laughter
Hair billowing out
Towards our two daughters
(One smirking, the other purposefully
Looking bored)
And there, in the window behind us
Just a glimmer
Of the middle-school novel
I wrote last year
Displayed on the cherrywood bookshelf
That I sanded and stained and shellacked
In the garage workshop
Of my dream house
The one with the turret
And tiny observatory
That lets me see, here in the early morning
All the things
I could have had.

FIREPIT FONDUE

You don't remember who it was
Who suggested we all move
From dinner table to back yard
As we make the easy spread of friendship
Each taking a spot around the blaze
Too bright to look at for too long
Like love

And now, put your hands on your belly
Or behind your head
Or in the soft touch of a lover
Laugh and let the light stay hazy
Things should never be too clear

Let the sounds settle
Crickets and the rush of a car somewhere
But mostly crackles and laughter
And voices talking over the flames
Others in hushed closeness
Or content silence
Each adding to the mix
Of this slowly melting night.

Boxing

I once faked an injury.

I was so good!
A football speedster
A superstar of the Texas suburbs
I fit, nice and snug in my place
For everyone else

I wish I'd had the strength
To break free
But who has that
At fifteen?

Not me!
And so I got out
The only way I could manage.

Today I try
Not to watch or listen
To commercials
Not to be lulled
By TV shows
And newscaster asides
Not to be shriveled
By social media posts

People still push
From every side
But sometimes, now
I have the strength
To push back.

SPRINT

Not a race against death
But a race with it

We're both gonna reach
The finish line at the same time

So let's head there headlong
Breathless
And full of life.

HELLO, HEART

Hello, heart, all shackles and shells
I want to set you loose
Practice "vulnerability"
And all the good words

But there is timing
And luck
And unforced errors
And there is time—

Both holding me down
And holding hope

Hello, heart, all shackles and shells
Perhaps today
Will finally be your day
And mine.

INVISIBLE INK

It's only at this time of night
Only after a few drinks
Only then will I tell you
Of the regret
Only then will I repeat
Those lines

The ones like rain prints on a window
That only show up
In just the right
Slant of light.

An Abundance of Annabels (a triptych)

Annabel I

The Spaghetti Warehouse is long gone
Maybe all of them are
But in its glory days
And mine
Was where I planned it out—
Just another casual meal between friends
We'd done lots of them
Taco Bell, the dorm cafeteria, walking between classes
"Let's do a fancy one!" I suggested to her
(So clever)
And over the fettuccine alfredo
Or maybe marinara with meatballs
I have no recollection of the actual food
But I do recall, with the clarity of a confessional
How I put down my fork
Cleared my throat
And told her that I felt
     No I wanted
     No we were destined
To be more than friends
After the longest pause
Her smile faded
It never quite returned the same
(For me at least)
That time is long gone
Which, like the Spaghetti Warehouse
Is probably for the best
But I am still glad we went there
When we could.

ANABEL 2

"You've got a spot of hummus
No, there, on the side of your mouth
No it's ... yes there you've almost—"
And then it fell from your face to the table
With a plop
I'm not sure what I expected
Perhaps a little embarrassing smile
A quick thank you
Or an "I can't believe I did that!"
Instead the whole courtyard lit up
With your laugh
And we somehow fell
Into easy conversation
Over light snacks and cold drinks
All the other law students
Left behind like that hummus
We watched *Grease* in your dorm room
That laugh of yours, each time
Was like peeking around the sun
Such good, good friends
Practically in orbit
But you had a boyfriend
And I never had the gravity
To ask
And so I was slung
Around your star
With a gentle push
Onto a different path.

BLOODLETTING (ANNABEL 3)

In the old days they used it
As a cure

I still remember
That frantic Valentine's night
I'd knocked, I'd called
Perhaps you were passed out inside
Or worse

I climbed the fence
Made my way to the window
Saw the room that I knew
By heart
The crumbly walls the dresser the chair
Where we sat together and recited *Macbeth*
("Out out, damn spot!")
The rug where Puck chewed his bone
The bed we shared—
And that's where you were.

With my hands cupped against the glass
It was like looking down a tunnel
Or at a flickering movie—
You, riding and writhing
On top of him

I felt the blood let
Felt everything
Drain away.

And we did try after that
A few times
But words and other acts
Of sincere apology
Could never quite out
That damned spot

Perhaps it was the cure
We both needed.

FAME

"Do you want to be famous?
Or do you want to be happy?"
Einstein asks me

I start to say both
But you can't fool Einstein

"Have some more wine"
Mussolini says
He's already sloppy drunk
Or maybe he's always like that?

I turn to ask Einstein
But he's buried in his work

"He only looks up once a week"
Joan of Arc tells me
Smiling as the blood drips down
"Just like when he was alive"

It's a grand feast
The ultimate round table
Knights and heroes
Stars of the screen and field
All the luminaries
No candles needed in here!

Joan is still smiling
"You have both," I tell her
She gestures a stained hand

Pele waives from a distance
Robin Williams, Marie Curie, Mother Theresa
Share a joke
Janis & Kurt are singing a duet
While Jesus plays the drums (who knew?)

"Yes," Joan says, "we all do now"
She gazes at the door
At the far end of the hall
"But not when it mattered."

PRUNING

My mom has no problem
She clips the roses
As soon as they droop
"But they still look good!" I say
"Need to make room for the new ones" she replies
I watch the bright flowers
Collect on the ground
And now the rose bush
Seems so bare

I go back inside
Weave around the boxes
Of old letters
That someday I will re-read
Slip on my threadbare PJs
That still fit so well
Even with the hole
Scoot the pile
Of To-Do lists to the side
Crack open a beer
Slide into the couch curve

Tomorrow is when
I will stop drinking
So much
I will hang that picture
I will go through those boxes
I will sort through
The decades of emails
I will stop looking at those old photos

Trying to put myself back there
Rather than right here

I will not go to Barton Springs Saloon
Again tonight
Instead I will get a good night's sleep
Wake up sober and refreshed
And start working on that writing project
The one that's been on all those To-Do lists
Piled on the table
For so long

Yes for sure
I will start pruning
Tomorrow.

CRACKED IS THE HEART

> *Cracked is the heart that might*
> *Have loved full well.*
> —Margaret Wise Brown

There is still time
It beats
There is still hope
It entreats

I have been broken
It thrums
But who has not?
It hums

My chamber is empty
It yearns
But more is to come
It churns

Even with cracks
It bleats
There is still hope
It repeats.

GHOSTS

The image flickers on a digital frame
A photo I'd forgotten
From decades ago
An unlined me
Caught in perpetual liminality

And I am pulled
Motionless
Across the room
Into the frame
Into the past
To the severe edge of longing

I am there and here
Laughing and overwhelmed
With grief

It takes all I have
To try to pull away
To come back to the here and hard-lined now
   I can't
      I just
         Can't

I power it off
That little slideshow window
To another world
And remind myself—
I don't believe in ghosts.

BEER FOAM ALL THE WAY DOWN

But what holds up the earth, wise one?
A turtle
And what holds up the turtle?
Another turtle
And below that?
It is turtles all the way down.
—unknown

I take a sip, set the mug back on the bar
It is half full, a line of broken foam across the top
I swirl it with my pinky
(It's okay, no one is watching)

In one spot
The foam spreads outward

I focus my gaze
Arrogantly
As if that single spot
Were the entirety
Of existence

Look! The universe
Is expanding!

In a pinky swirl of foam
Atop a bottomless sea.

Here's a Brochure to Explain That Poem

Three drinks in
I can see the pattern now
It's totally—
Wait let me get my phone
Take a photo so I don't—
Shit the beer moved
But you can still kind of make out the little demon
Floating in the foam across the top
That part there is a bouquet, or maybe a leaf
I can see them all
Dispersing
Or contracting
Depending on where you are
And really that's what I meant
That's the secret—
There is no Big Bang
There is only the perspective
Of the moment you can measure
Of the tiny twirl
You're in.

TENDER

Tender is the soul
In change
Tender is the life
Rearranged

It is so much safer
To not pull at seams
Ah but to live!
Is to painfully tug
                At dreams.

I Want a Holographic Display

The guy up ahead
Younger than me
From the look of his bouncy stride
His bouncy hair
All the bounce
That guy, headed my direction
I bet he just started his run

I am near the end of mine
And this downhill part
Is harder on the knees
At the start, though
I was almost as bouncy

I want it lit up
In flashing letters above me as he passes by—
      "I've done six miles already!"
      "I was up all night for a deadline!"
      "Last month I banged my knee"
      "I am trying to quit my job"
      "My parents divorced
      When I was four"

Maybe then bouncy guy would understand
Why I'm so sluggish right now

And yes, okay
Maybe he can have a display
For me not to judge
Either.

BEING 50 IS NOTHING!

Haha bring me cake!
Haha bring me beer!
Being fifty is nothing!
It is only a year!

A bite of jealousy
A swallow of fear
A look back at twenty—
Now *that* was a year!

With neckline so smooth
And tendons that heal
I am long past that
But not done with my meal!

So give me more cake!
Pour one more beer!
Being fifty is *today*!
And today is my year.

Broken (from the bottom up)

having given up all hope
  "she died a broken soul"

having ended
  "their marriage was broken long before"

having been damaged and no longer in working order
  "seeing him that night, her heart was broken"

denoting a promise not kept
  "only one vow was broken"

spoken falteringly, as if overflowing with emotion or mistakes
  "he proposed in broken English"

having breaks or gaps in continuity
  "laughing, they drew a broken line in the sand and laid
  down"

having an uneven and rough surface
  "his world swayed when they met, as if stumbling on
  broken ground"

denoting a family in which the parents are divorced or separated
  "she came from a broken home"

DOLORES O'RIORDAN

Still
The best show I've ever seen

They were considered pop
But on that day
1994 at the Warfield in San Francisco
The Cranberries simply rocked
Strewn across the stage
Guitars clanging in unison
Drums shaking paint flakes from walls
And that voice—

Pure raw energy
Emotion funneled
From mouth to microphone to speakers
To me
More powerful than I ever
Could have imagined
Just like her death.
How could someone
Born the same year as me
Be gone?

Yes, there is the arc of the dive
Then the slip beneath
But still
Forever above the waves
Still
And always—
That voice.

RAINBOW PUPPY JOYTIMES!

Because you can't be down
Every single moment
Even drudgery
Takes a break.

SOMETIMES THAT'S ALL YOU GET
(AN ODE TO CATE)

There is no lasting happiness in this world,
only particles of happiness.
—Michael Simms

Be thankful you knew her at all.
—Dido

I want to freeze it
That sliver when she and I were thick as thieves
Stealing away for texts and calls
Doubling, tripling over with laughter
When there was all the possibility in the world
In that sly crooked smile
My hope rising at the corners too

That possibility is long gone
But every so often
I play it on repeat—
Those brief flashes
Those light and star-filled times
When even a glimmer
Was enough.

AND THEN IT'S DONE

To my kids:

You just get one shot
And then it's done
No do-overs
No save-for-laters
No "wow that crept up on me!"s

I wish I'd been told
To marry young
Have kids younger
Rather than told how rash it was
Even though everyone else
Had done it

I wish I'd been told to start each day
With what I'd be most proud of
Rather than save it for after
Grading papers.

I never had kids.

Rain

The rain is coming down
Let it wash or drown you—
Your choice.

TRULY KNOWN

You have seen my tantrums
Seen my bald spots and frequent naps
You have heard my fears
And long-buried lies
You have endured the smells
The just-off jokes
The time I forgot to ask
About your big presentation
The sins and shaky
Apologies
You have endured it all
And yet still
You stay.

BURL

I have hope
It will turn out
Breathtaking
I have pride
I won't burn out
Yet shaking
I carve and peel back
I starve to feel that
Knot naked and exposed
Not faking and clothed

I worry my bumpy burls
Will hurry this thumping world
To judge my outsides
To fudge my downsides
Still I'll let you inside
See this whimpering new side
This broken and glued side
This shattered and true side
This oh I've been through side
This pain shame and bruised side

This
This will be
A pulsing lifeforce
A dull thing brought forth
A swirling pattern
Of love tattered
Of dreams dashed
Of dreams passed

And yet
Still
And yet
Still

There is none other like it
So curl your lip and dislike it
Or with love embrace it
For with love I trace it
Imperfectly grand
With still shaking hand
This burl, sublime
This world, mine.

I Just Want to Grab Everything Good

Hold it near
Before a friend slips away forever
Keep these wild moments and live them
Again
Maybe that's why the leaf spins
Outstretched
As it falls.

To Steven

You are crying
Do you remember?
Ten, fifteen years ago
On the phone
You telling me
About the cancer
In your leg
I was pulled over in my car
Both of us still so young
I doubt if I'd ever heard you cry
Before that
I was scared
Too
"What if I never get to see
My daughter grow up?" you asked
There was no answer
There is none
I sat there parked
You sobbed

It was so long ago
You are fine now, all cancer free
(Though with that limp)
Ella is grown
Sometimes I am afraid of being alone
Not feeling loved
You could have called anyone that night
You called me
"Thanks," you said as you hung up
And is what I say back
All the time.

POUR-OVER COFFEE

There is a proper way—
Do not dump all the water at once
You're not putting out a fire

Do not drip like a sieve
You're not protecting faucets from a freeze

No, this is a liquid art
The first pour, just after the boil subsides
Is a gentle circle
Almost as if you are massaging the grounds

As if, after a long drought
You are readying a patch of garden
For a new start

Yes, just like that—
Feel the coffee soak it in
Hear the bubbles of delight

Now, wait.
Do not rush.

Nothing blossoms
In an instant.

Give it time to bind
Molecule to molecule
Yes, just like that—ah, sweet symbiosis!
Now the lush loam is ready.

Pour the rest tenderly
A steady rain around the edges
Working toward the center

They call it the bloom—
This waking moment, right now
When the flavor reaches
Its peak.

STRANGER

It's in the videos
The neck, in particular
When did those strains and folds
Appear?
When did age
Streak in
Like lines
In a photo
Of someone else?

ODE TO THE CLOSED PUB

Like a thousand voices suddenly cried out, then nothing.
—Obi Wan Kenobi

It is not Alderaan
Being smashed to space rocks
But still
This corner
Has been the site
Of wedding proposals
And breakups
Of one-night stands sparked
And lifelong friendships kindled

It has been the raucous laughter drowning out
For a while at least
The demons
It has been the quiet comfort
Of not being alone
Of always having a space
Without questions
Or judgmental looks.

And so
When you show up one night
And the sign is taped to the door
And there is nothing inside
But a few coasters, scattered like space rocks

No, it is not Alderaan
It is real.

LOST FOREVER

Metropolis
You know, the old movie
Have you seen it?
Well, not all of it, of course
No one alive today has

They lost it
Lost frames and bits of film
Whoosh disintegrated!
To irretrievable dust

And *Doctor Who*?
The early episodes, some of them
Completely gone!

But they're still okay, I guess
Choppy *Metropolis* is better than none
And isn't *Doctor Who*
About time gaps anyway?

I have all these photos I need to organize
All my music I need to put
In one easily-accessible place
All these poems to write, places to visit
Before it is all lost forever!

"You can't have everything,"
My therapist reminds me
"And you're still much more
Than okay."

SHOW DON'T TELL

The world will not pause
For your list of dreams
You have to hack through the disinterested jungle
Every single time
Every single day

So pick up your sword
Your pen
Your smile
And show us all.

THE HOUSE OF THE TRAGIC POET

Although the size of the house itself is in no way
remarkable, its interior decorations are of the highest
quality and variation among others from ancient Pompeii.
—Wikipedia

I keep meaning to visit
They say it is a jumble
A hodge-podge of mosaic floors and frescoes
Art from all periods and places
As if the Library of Alexandria
Were kept in a plain simple shack
Art upon art upon art
Tucked in Hermione's purse

No one knows
Who built it, owned it
It is forever frozen in wisps of ash
Out of tragedy comes beauty?
Or something like that
Anyway, I don't think the owners
Were hoping for anything like this
They just wanted to keep living
To walk outside another day

I will try to remember that
As I fret about my words and dreams tucked in here
Maybe someone will find them
When I am floating ash

Maybe I should just go out
Enjoy the day while I can.

GATHERING RAIN

I scribble an idea on a post-it note
So fast I can hardly read my own writing!
But that's okay, it's such an important one
That I'm sure I'll remember enough
To decipher it later

I drop the note atop all the others
Waiting in the mahogany box
That I stained and lacquered myself
Such a gorgeous place
To keep the future

But for now I have to go!
I hurry into the storm
The raindrops sliding from my jacket
Into the dirt

Of course I do not try to catch them
To sprinkle on the ground later
Ha!
Who would do that?

DUSK

Are you a beach
Or mountains person?
The dating app asks

Where is the option
For this—
A snow-covered field in the biting cold
Things are never this clear anywhere else

The crunch of my footsteps
The steam of my breath
Wind creaking the trees
Bare birch rubbing against maple
Like woodblocks

The sun a sliver
Sinking through skeleton limbs
Lower, then lower still

I am drawn to it, all this
Like a moth
To the moon.

ORIGINAL

Scribble those lines at 2:23 a.m.
Then cross them out
Remind yourself—
> *This has all been done before.*
> *I am a hack.*

All true
Dylan was a hack
DaVinci stole

Now pause
Consider the word
Original—
Not a genesis from the void
But a returning to the well, to the origin
For more

Now realize
That nothing grows
From nothing
Even the Big Bang
Traces farther (and further) back
So do not fret for freshness
Embrace the harvest
Add your words and swirls
Scribble those lines, and remind yourself—
> *Nothing is completely new*
> *This is my beautiful minutiae mixed in*
> *My tiny*
> *Stardust spin.*

MEAL FROM THE STAFF

You can say
I come here too much
This bar, this spot, this stool
Order the same thing
Every time
But there is also something to be said
For security
For making the same jokes
With the bartender, cooks, manager
For listening
Smiling and nodding
For buying them a drink on the sly
For simply settling into this worn wood seat
Where even hardness
Can comfort.

And so when there is one meal leftover
From those cooked for the staff
And it is given to me—
Yes it is delicious
But that is not what matters
It warms more, and deeper
Than all those whiskeys ever could.

THINGS NOT CARRIED

It is bulk collection day
I haul out the rattan chair
That I got from Pier One in my twenties

Kaitlyn said I would outgrow it
Or it would break within a year
Ha, showed you, Kaitlyn!

It was a good chair
Though not for sex
As Victoria and I discovered
Twice

It wobbles as I set it beside the curb
I wonder what Kaitlyn would think
Or Victoria

I go back inside
Alone
My shoulders sagging
From all I have left.

GHOST

I have been here
In this spot
—yes exactly the one you are looking at right now—
For so long

And despite appearances
I am still very much alive
And wanting

Yes there is a hardening
That comes with age
A clouding of vision

But perhaps you
Will not be so affected?
Perhaps you
Will not walk so swiftly by?

Perhaps you
—someone, anyone—
Will finally take the time
To see.

I Wanted to Write the Best Poem

Wanted to please all the critics
Soar metaphors! Slant truths!
Plant universally-specific and instantly-relatable details
Then wait till it blossomed to pithy perfection
To put it on the page.

But this life
Is the only one I have.

A Form of Emptying

Up on the stage
There was no waiting for tomorrow
He would pull the microphone close
Like a lover on a last date
And howl

Dripping sweat
—blink and keep going—
Blinding lights
—blink and keep going—

Tell a joke between songs
Then rip into a soaring lament
Dance a dirge
Pour it all out
From self to stage to the parched fans
—drink and drink and drink!—

Clutch the microphone for the final song
Drenched and drained and spent
Barely holding on
But knowing the secret—
The well always
Refills.

GAHANNA FIELD

There's a spot in the Lake District
A winding stretch of dirt road
Overlooking rolling hills and a distant stream
A plaque says Wordsworth
Long ago proclaimed it the most beautiful view
In all of England

Here in central Ohio
Is the sagging chain link fence
The spotty baseball field
Flanked by the Dairy Queen
That hasn't changed its marquee in decades

After one Little League game
The players lifted me onto their shoulders
Carried me off that field
And we all got dipped cones and Blizzards

I slow my car as I pass the old spot
I am not Wordsworth
And do not need to be
To make my own proclamations
To put up plaques
Wherever I damn please.

RESILIENCE
for Shayna

The pieces break
And fall
Those scrimshaw etchings
Of who you wanted the world to see
Shatter
And you are left
Raw
Trembling
Unsure
And you can scramble
To pick them up
To try and reassemble
      Or

You can step forward
Hear that old shell crunch
Underfoot
And realize that the you
Inside
The true
Fiercely tender
Beautifully imperfect
You
Has always been there
Just waiting to be seen
And is so much stronger
Than you ever
Could have dreamed.

STAINED

Do not look
The sun head-on
It is best seen
Just before dawn

When that smile
Bold and bright
Reveals its truth
In more subtle light

Do not be fooled
By the confident stride!
A wayward soul
Trembles inside

Do not think you
Are the only one!
There is darkness
In every sun

Nothing is pure
Or truly free
The stained light is what
You need to see.

STAIRWELL, DRUNK, 12:03AM

Every little
Corner portion
Of our lives
Is crafted by
Someone.

LAMENTING THE LOSS OF A PUB

Ah the Gingerman in its glory!
The regulars clustered at the bar corner
Sure there's room for one more!
The beam of polished wood
Holding us all up—
Meri, exhausted from a day on her feet
Buck, weary from a life of law
Shylo, needing support from a breakup
Dave, a creature of habit
It is close to Christmas
And behind the long row of beer taps
Are stockings with each of our names
The rest of the bar turns at our laughter burst
We are so loud!
And I am not ashamed

Today I ran into Meri at the vintage store
It had been 10 years, at least
All the store customers turned at our greeting
We were so loud!

The Gingerman now is rubble
Beneath a parking lot and condos
I feel the pull each time I drive by
And I am sad, oh yes
But I am never
Ashamed.

ROOTS

They are like giants, these trees
Splitting sidewalks
Throwing concrete
In slow motion

I hurry over the angled slabs along my path
Though it's not really—
I didn't lay it

I pause mid-tilt
Wondering
If I should stay on this cracked square
Someone else made
For someone else
Or perhaps leap off!
Or perhaps stomp it
To dust.

Wondering if there is the DNA
Of giants
Somewhere deep
In me.

SOMETHING BETTER

still waiting for
something better
—unknown

Better to leap and have something
Imperfect
To work with
      Build upon
            Nurture into

Than have those words
On your grave.

THREE SPOTS

They were just there one afternoon—
Boom
An itch and then
Huh, look at that

Maybe that is how it happens—
One day fresh and smooth and itch-free
And the next old

For some it's a gradual aging
For me it was three spots
Sprouting up
On the back of my hand
On a Tuesday.

BENEDICTION (A HAIKU)

In celebration
Of coffee, sunlight, nice pens
Little things, are not.

LINES WRITTEN IN EARLY WINTER

after *"Lines Written in Late Spring"*
by *William Wordsworth*

In that bleak mood when bitter thoughts
Bring warm thoughts to the mind
I touch the window still with frost
And let the past unwind...

That sweet first crunch!
That blue-seared sky!
I'll stop this hand
And go outside...

I'll sink in deep!
That fresh new snow!
I'll stop this window-gazing
I'll stop one day, I know.

GOLDEN GOOSE

I never quite got into Terry Pratchett
I mean, I wanted to, he seems exactly
Up my reader alley

On the barstool next to me
This guy is hunched over
A paperback copy of Pratchett's *Discworld*
Open in front of him

The chatter is loud
Here at the Golden Goose on a Saturday night
On the other side of the bar
A couple is making out
They could be doing that in private
Just like the guy reading beside me

I sip my beer
Try to swallow a bit of judgment too

They're not hurting anyone I guess
Well, the couple could be a little less risqué
On the eyes
But still

Maybe it's just the feeling
Of belonging
In whatever way you can

I take another sip
That, I get.

What I Wish I'd Been Told

A storm will come
They always do
And so tether yourself
  —Now, not tomorrow—
One person is enough
More than enough
And there is no wrong
Except waiting and weighing out
Your options
Tethering only means mutual trust
The faith that you will both hold on

And it may break
(Like I have shown you many times)
But then trust and hold again

The only wrong
Is waiting and weighing
The endless choices
Because when the storm comes
  —It always does—
When the storm comes
All the weighing
Will sink you.

Unbroken Solitude

Creative work needs solitude.
—Mary Oliver

Human beings are wired
For connection
I have read it, heard it
A hundred times

I dip my brush
In cadmium yellow
Maybe I'll start today
With some brightness

But no, that would be too
Van Gogh
Or perhaps mistaken
For Dali

The artists, the true humans
Must forge their own path
I have read it, heard it
A hundred times

And so this is why I do not answer the door
Why I cringe at small or large talk
I am wired for connection, yes
But I will not let that break me.

CONSTRUCTION (GRAVITY, DEATH, LOVE)

Time is one—
A construct of made-up minutes
A tree knows nothing of seconds
Only the sun and shifting seasons
Even past and future
Are bendy as Einstein's logic

Math?
An ant does not know numbers
Or long division

Words?
These letters are only swirls in your mind
Across the world this same word
Is a pile of sticks
Stacked by someone else

Religion & republics
Democracies & demons
Borders & the concept
Of breakfast

From wearing a shirt
To owning a home
Investing, retiring
Pretending to like golf

All built—
Should by should
Ad by ad

Instructional book
By disapproving look
Over millennia
Not all construction
Is progress

So there is gravity
        There is death
                There is love
None of which
You can truly escape

But the rest?
Oh for everything else
The building blocks
Are all yours.

WAVING GOODBYE

I don't remember the first time she did it
Perhaps it was when I left for college
But it is exactly the same today
As decades ago—

I am backing out of the driveway
Of my childhood home
As she waves

I am putting the car in drive, moving forward
As she walks across the front yard
Keeping pace with me, and waves

I am pausing at the corner of the street
Looking back
She is so tiny now
Moving to the very edge of the yard
Where she puts her hand even higher, and waves
So that I can see her, through tears
One last time.

Leave the Door Open for the Dark

It was my recurring nightmare as a kid—

I'm at our apartment complex
Being chased across the parking lot
Then into our building
Then up the stairs to my room
My legs heavier with each step

If I don't reach my door first
Don't make it inside
Before being caught
I'll never
Wake up

I don't know why
I let that haunt me so long
I don't know why
It took until now
For me to stop running
And turn.

To-Do at 51

Clear the unread emails
From twenty years
Take a match
To the notebooks of story ideas
Keeping me buried
In possibility

Dredge
Then level the heaps
Into flat and fertile ground
Where I can finally see
The horizon
Where I can finally have room
To breathe
And be.

PLEASING

Others
To please yourself
Until too late
You realize
You never liked
Vanilla.

X

"See you at trivia, babe!"
I had forgotten how we called each other babe
"I love you!"
I'd forgotten saying that to her, too
I should delete all these old texts
I really should

But we are not enemies
Still friends I think
Mild acquaintances at least

I take another sip of gin, keep scrolling
An ex is just a crossroads, I remind myself
Not a collision!
An ex is

Simply   the point
  where   both
    our   lives
      met
   got   tangled
and   stuck

Until one of us broke free

Yes I really should delete these texts
Definitely definitely not send a new one

But it has been a bad day
And I have forgotten
A lot.

Are the Headlights Getting Brighter?

I squint
Like a deer
Caught, frozen
In oncoming
Age.

IMPRESSIONS

Out for a jog
Left knee stiff
Muscles long
Past their peak

When was that?
My twenties? Maybe thirty?
When did it go from building up
To just slowing
The leak?

Behind me is the hum of an approaching car
I pick up my pace
Ignore my left knee
Raise my shoulders, shake out my hands
As if to show the car, *This is nothing!*
As if to show everyone, *I'm only halfway done!*

The car passes.
It is nobody I know.
It never is.

When it is out of sight
I slow to my age
And my left knee sighs
Like my therapist—
Who are you trying
To impress?

THAT SAYING

The funny thing is
You think you have time.
—unknown

I make the lists
Of dreams—

Of books read
Of partner found
Of children reared with gleaming eyes
Watching as I pore through my boxes
Of old school papers and laughing photos
That ones that I kept just for this moment—

To remind those dreams
What the funny thing is
Again.

I Wish I Had the Right Words

I wish I could tell you
The pain will slip mossy soft
Into a thin layer you wear
Without noticing
I wish I could tell you
How gloriously love will crush again
How exquisite the new drowning

I wish I could let you see
How we are all trembling
How we all want so so much
To belong
Without smothering

I wish I could share
Like the health points
Above a player in a video game
What your level really is

I wish I could tell you
Of bent grass days
Of the worth of clouds
Of choosing touch

I wish I had the words
The right ones
To tumble in
Soothe the midnight fears
And show you it is never
Too late.

STOPPING BY A WELL ON A SNOWY EVE

after *"Stopping by Woods on a Snowy Evening"*
by *Robert Frost*

Whose well this is I do not care!
They may see me stop and stare
But likely there is no one here—
Just this well beyond repair.

Something about it draws me near
Intrigue with a mix of fear
I wonder when last it turned
And if its water still is clear.

When I was younger oh I yearned!
For love so deep, so deep it burned!
But I never stopped, I just ran
And now in winter I am spurned.

This crank is cold in my hand
I always thought I had a plan
But I am still a lonely man
But I am still a lonely man.

LUCKY

Even in the dark morning hours
The ones where I should be sleeping
But instead kick at the jumble of sheets
Feel my shirt pushed up too high
By my too-fat belly

Even here, alone with worry
Even here, I must remember
The soft bed I have
The sturdy walls and roof
The loves I have had under other walls and roofs
The faces I have been lucky enough
To share time with

Not now, of course
But still
I count the celebrations
Like fireflies
Telling me to sleep
Just sleep
Let the softness take you
The joy will glow
Again.

P.S. Private Party! (around back)

I wanted to invite everyone
A party for you and for you—
The downtrodden
Mingled with the uplifted

A small cake
Sparkly hat
Balloons of hope
For all

Just come right around back!
Maybe you'll find a friend
Or make one
Or just quietly find a spot
To belong
Which isn't that really
The best gift of all?

I wanted to invite everyone!
I really did.

MY FAVORITE MISTAKE

When she smiles
Her eyes disappear
I used that in a poem for her once

Now I drive away
Away from Athens, away from her
The Ohio highway cuts a path through the trees
And I put in a Sheryl Crow CD

It was a grand plan—
Show up at her work (surprise!)
Confess my change of heart
Say I want to try again

I did all that
Then we stood beside her Jeep
Just like we had back in college
But with a bit more distance

"I'm engaged," she said
"But not married," I said, repeating my mom's words
She laughed, eyes disappearing

"Would you have done this," she asked
"If you really thought I'd say yes?"
And I wanted to protest
Wanted to show I'd changed.

Her smile was kind as I drove off
And it deserves more poems
But not from me.

POUR IT ALL OUT

Should you save it for later?
For your urn?
For the ashes as they are poured, swirling
To the winds and water?
Is that when you will wait
To do your dance?

I Am a Perfectly Flawless Diamond

There are odes
To the rough
There are tributes
To the tough

There are hymns
About growth and improvement
Tony Robbins will tell you
Life is all about movement

But sometimes I stop
And just look in the mirror
Today is fucking perfect
Right now and right here.

To Boldligo

I was a kid, maybe six or seven
Watching the *Star Trek* opening credits
And there was the USS *Enterprise*
Gliding through outer space
Who wouldn't lean closer to the TV?

And—whoosh!—as it slid by
Whose head wouldn't turn?
As if I could follow it
Into the stars

Ah, and then those lofty words:
"These are the voyages... of the Starship *Enterprise*...
To boldly go...
Where no one has gone before!"

Only in my entranced state
I mistakenly heard, "To Boldligo..."
And then of course who wouldn't wonder:
"Boldligo? What planet is *that*?"
And, each episode, lean in, heart pounding
Hoping *this* will be it—
The time I finally get to go
Where no one else has...

I am not giving up.
And there are no mistakes.

WHAT ARE THESE POEMS IN MY HEAD?

Are they more, or less,
If I keep them there?
To be seen and heard—
Is that what makes words real?
Worth it?

Substitute *life*
For *words*.

I am awake, mid-night
The time of dust-covered souls
When mine screeches loudest

I wonder if ancient poets
Played back their choices in the dark
If they had these same reels on repeat
Keeping them from sleep

And so what is there to do
In these panicky dust times?
You cannot go back
As much as fantasy calls, lulls
It is less than a wisp of mist

And so the insomniac's dream
Of changing what is past
This dream must fall (please)
Into its own sleep
A silent lament is needed, yes,
A cleansing sort of grief
And I do love a good cleaning

But I can only vacuum the same spot for so long
Before I must get up and go out
Into a world
That will always be dusty

And so, what *is* there to do?
Move forward (others cannot)
Spread just one smile (some cannot even do that)
Just one kind word to a stranger on the street
Across a bar
Or in the mirror

So yes, panic and clean for a bit, as we all must
Then share your words!
Free-flowing and mistake-filled!
Substitute *life* for... Here, I'll start—

> *The dust that was*
> *Long before us*
> *Stars and silence*
> *And all that fuss*
>
> *The dust we are*
> *In the glowing now*
> *And will become*
> *Doesn't matter how*
>
> *What can you do?*
> *Just dance in your mote*
> *Celebrate until*
> *That's all she wrote.*

BUSINESS

The business of life is the acquisition of memories.
In the end that's all there is.
—Carson, *Downton Abbey*

I hope he's wrong.
Memories are slick and fickle—
My mom tells me the same story
She did earlier in the call.

I do not think life is a ledger
Of debits and credits
To look back on
No thank you, Carson
I prefer the business
Of forgotten starbursts and passing whimsy
Of silent times alone, acquiring nothing
Of celebrating the mundane photos
Not taken

The only choice we can make
Ever
Is the one we did
Then

And in the end, Carson?
In the end there is the starburst
And what comes after that
No one really remembers.

WHO DID I THINK I WAS FOOLING?

Buying that candy and chocolate
To save
For tomorrow?

Dinner Party

You have spent years
Preparing for this!
The perfect outfit
The newest dish!

Now take a seat
At this sumptuous table
Yes that's your chair!
It has your label

Not written by *you*
Ha you would never!
You are not that skilled
Nor that clever

Just sit there and smile
You are sure to please!
With your style and grace
And willing ease

To wear the right clothes
To say the right thing
(And even when you hate it
To loudly sing)

There are other choices
You could have made
But then you would not
Be *here* today!

At this lovely table
Set by others
Far be it from you
To ever discover

That you have passed
On what you deserve—
That you have spent your life
On the hors d'oeuvres.

The Good (Grasping)

This right here
This shared whiskey
This springtime sun
This tossing the ball with the dog
Back and forth
This easy conversation
Nothing forced or fake
And yet why do I yearn
Always
For the impossibility
Of more?

LETTING GO

We all do it
Try and chase down
That stray balloon
Tromp through mud, slip and fall
Scraping our knees and heart
On gravel
Telling ourselves
It's worth it
Telling ourselves
All this pain and struggle
Will be so so minimal
Once that floating red prize
Is ours

And so we run
Run and run and run
Avoid the advice of others
And ourselves
Until finally, as that bit of red
Disappears in the distance
We realize it was never meant
For us
That it never wanted
To be caught.

BACK-ALLEY PROPOSALS

I am down on one knee in the sludge
Behind the bar
So so drunk

It is forgotten the next day
Except not by her, 20 years later:
"Remember the time you proposed"
She says with a smile
That hides a hundred fears

Today, I found an old To-Do list tucked in a book
Last year, when I moved
I discovered a *Murder at Mystery Oaks!* party game
Unopened

I smile back at her
And there is a moment...

"I'm glad we're still friends," I finally say
And remind myself that things put off
Long enough
Are never meant to be.

HOPE

is a leaf on the wind
is a bubble on a wave
is asking
       um, hey
         do you wanna
         dance?

is opposable thumbs
forming from stardust

is the ground looming
after each leap
yet still saying yes
         oh yes
         what a ride!

WRINKLES

When I was ten
I bought a basket of baseball cards
In mint condition
But they looked too new
To be worth anything
So I crinkled them up
Made a huge crease across
Cal Ripken's rookie face
There, I thought
Now they have value

How is it
That I've forgotten that
Today?

Let's Do It Again!

"It was a fine trip," my mom tells me in our Sunday call
"But my friend Gabby is already planning to go back—
rent the same house, visit all the same places.
She always wants to recreate every good moment.
But you can't."

My mom had probably said that before
But mom advice is often unheeded
The first 52 times.

But this time I realized
I'd been Gabby, all these years—
Doing the same road trip
As the first great one
Trying to re-cook
That perfect dinner

Later that day, my neighbor says she's worried
About selling her house:
"What if I want to move back here?" she says
"In a few years?"

"You can't," I reply
Surprising us both
"It will never be the same."

Funny how moms can still teach you things
No matter how old
You both are.

Lists

I have made all the lists:
- What I'm grateful for
- Times I felt loved
- Projects I'm super-proud of!

All the things I need right now
To soothe the silent screams
At 3:00am
To push me out of bed
At 8:00am
To catch the one-two punch
Of failure and fear
On a sunny afternoon

I have done all that
And in this bright moment
Reading the lists
The happiness oversweeps

But I know.

I know.

Just a Touch of Lonely

I'm okay most of the time, I just feel a little lonely tonight.
—Tom Petty

Sit with it
Let it tremble beside you
This lonely is only
Looking to be held
Even for a fraction of a touch
Of a moment

Sit with it
Invite it to share its deepest fears
Listen together—
To the soft calls
Of silence
Of the grave
Of midnight murmurs

"Do not live for the grave"
(Whisper this)
"There cannot be love and touch every hour"
(You would smother)
(And be itchy)
"Hope will return
Just like dawn always does"
(Whisper this, too)

Sit with it, ask it to take your hand
In this fraction
Of a touch
Of a moment.

ROOFTOP SILENCE

It's where people come
For their last moments
There are other ways of course
Jump in front of a train, car, any moving machine
But here
You are the only movement
I could never do it
But still I dangle my legs
There is no sound
The sun is just a pale blue wave
Hours before the actual rise
It's my favorite time
The slightest shiver of pink
And then a chirp
A bustle
The row of birds (I have no idea what kind)
On the power line nearby
They have been perched too
And we all swivel
Toward the smudge of rising light
Now there is a small chattering
Perhaps excitement at what's to come
I don't know bird sounds or songs
But this is not offensive
Not what it will be like
When that sun does rise
When the machines start building
When the cars and trucks rush
When the noise drowns out nature
I could never do it
But here, right now, on this perch

With the slow silence, the not-unpleasant birdsongs
Is not the worst choice, I guess
For your last place to fly.

WHAT I HAVE FOUND

I have found that saying yes leads to growth
That growth is painful
That stagnancy is easy
That we all fear the same things
Every day
No matter how far along we are
That society makes it hard if you don't jump the hoops—
Kids, spouse, homeowner
But you can belong just as much without having done
Any of those
Or so I hope

I have found that hope
Above all
Is the daily challenge
I have found that saying yes is what stirs hope
And that the smallest flutter
Is all you need
To find.

LITTLE FREE LIBRARY

Mine is not just books
Not just this wooden box
(Though it is a fine piece of craftsmanship
Thank you very much)

Mine is also this lantana
I planted in the spring—
Go ahead, take a long look
Borrow as much as you want

Mine is also this Monkey Puzzle tree
That was here long before I came along
But I still tend to
As if I'm its caretaker—
Go ahead, touch the bark
Marvel at the upwards fireworks
Of its jagged leaves
There is no due date

These poems are yours
And everyone's—
Go ahead
Check them out.

WEST TEXAS STARS

I took a trip
To west Texas
By myself
Pulled over at night
On a stretch nowhere near McDonald
Or Ft. Davis
And just walked a long while
The sound
Of my feet on sand
That hadn't been touched
In perhaps centuries

And I never looked up
Only down
Focusing my gaze
Picking out one
Tiny
Twinkling grain
Whispering
You
      Too
           Are seen.

It's Not Much

Maybe you'll stop
Pause in your flurry
Maybe you'll find
A respite from worry

Maybe one poem
One single line
Will make you whisper
"That's just like mine."

Like that driver who slows
To give you the lane
Like that unrequited smile
When you're in pain

Change comes about
In the smallest of ways
How you spend your seconds
Is how you live your days

So here in these words
It's not much, I suspect
But we do what we can
To briefly connect.

THERE'S NOTHING THERE

Just a blink of New Mexico highway—
A washed-out flat
A piece of plywood
That used to be the start
Of something

Dirt and rocks and scrub
That gully
And tiny mile marker
Telling me
What tenth of nowhere
I'm in

Why do I remember all that—
That passing glimpse
Among thousands
Even better than Santa Fe's spiraling
Staircase church?

Maybe it's hope
That these words, too
Won't be forgotten.

Every Step

Don't mourn the paths not taken
Or the paths that never were
Revel in the road ahead—
Step forth excited! And unsure!

Acknowledgements

I am extremely grateful to the editors of the following publications, in which two poems in this book first appeared:

- *Writing Gifts* (Austin Bat Cave anthology): "To Steven"
- *Texas Observer* magazine: "West Texas Stars"

A huge thank you also to:

- Owen & Jodi Egerton, for all the front-yard whiskey chats, several of which sparked ideas for these poems; and Owen for the kind blurb words as well
- Carrie Fountain, for your input on a few of these poems in your workshop, and your sparkling support overall
- Sarah Orman, Jen Ryen, and Christian Goldstagg, our wonderful little group from Carrie's workshop—still meeting when we can!—for your suggestions on several poems in here
- Naomi Shihab Nye, for making me believe I'm a poet
- Rebecca Bendheim, for being my first reader and strongest cheerleader—your enthusiasm is contagious!— oh and hey for also coming up with the original cover idea!
- my entire Typewriter Rodeo family, for being on this poetry adventure together for over a decade now
- Andrea Wofford & Shanna Gerlach for your cover design magic
- Sarah Beach for your meticulous copyediting skills
- and Mom & Dad, for your never-ending support in all my creative (and other) endeavors.

SEAN PETRIE is an award-winning poet, author, and professor. He is a founder of the nationally-renowned Typewriter Rodeo poetry group and his recent books include *Typewriter Rodeo* (Andrews McMeel), *Listen to the Trees* (Documentary Media; IPPY silver medal), *Pet Poems* (Burlwood; IPPY bronze medal), the *Pet Poems Plus* workbook (Burlwood; Moonbeam Children's Book Award), and the *Jett Ryder* series for kids (JollyFish Press).

Sean does weekly radio poems for Texas NPR and his poetry has appeared in the *The Dallas Morning News, Texas Observer*, and *Beacon West* magazine, among others. He teaches legal writing at the University of Texas School of Law and has an MFA in Writing for Children from Vermont College of Fine Arts. Born in Ohio, he has been a longtime resident of Austin, but is often found traveling around (and exploring pubs in) Seattle and New England.

www.SeanPetrie.com

Front cover design by Andrea Wofford

Back cover design by Andrea Wofford & Shanna Gerlach

Front cover illustration from French magazine L'Illustration, No 2481, September 13, 1890, titled "The Patrie hot air balloon falling 1400 metres, Paris, France," housed in the museum Biblioteca Ambrosiana, Milan, Italy (artist unknown)

Back cover photo by Brad Marcum

Interior typeset in Adobe Gil Sans and Garamond

Cover typeset in Faune and October Condensed

BURLWOOD BOOKS

Burlwood Books is a small,
independent press in Austin, Texas.
We are dedicated to art that celebrates
the messy, vibrant, mistake-filled
wonder of life.

www.BurlwoodBooks.com